GOING WILD

Wild Nature

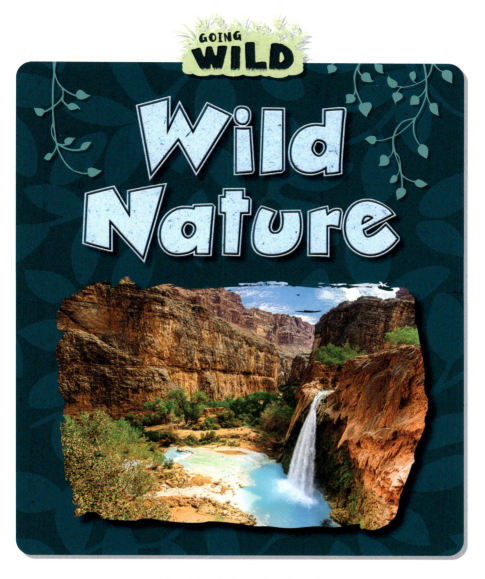

by Noah Leatherland

Minneapolis, Minnesota

Credits
All images courtesy of Shutterstock. With thanks to Getty Images, Thinkstock Photo, and iStockphoto. Recurring images – Very_Very, Barbara.M.Mattson, Apostrophe, ArtKio, Ton Photographer 4289. Cover – pashabo, WinWin artlab, Hibrida, Potapov Alexander, Svetlana Parshakova, Gizele. 2–3 – lukaszemanphoto. 4–5 – Abbe Daryant, Beth Ruggiero-York, Eric Isselee, Ortis, svsumin. 6–7 – BlueBarronPhoto, CrizzyStudio, Peeradontax, Vector Insanity. 8–9 – Madlen, Arlee.P, Eric Isselee, Kokhanchikov, Michiel de Wit, Rudmer Zwerver, SAKDA NARATHIPWAN, YueStock. 10–11 – Everett Collection, Kletr, Krasula, lusia83, Tatiana Grozetskaya, Vova Shevchuk. 12–13 – Anna Frajtova, Designer things, Hey swift. 14–15 – Alody, alvarobueno, Tony Skerl, trancedrumer. 16–17 – 8H, Hlib Shabashnyi, Kononova Nina, Martin Grossman. 18–19 – Calin Stan, iliuta goean, Irina Wilhauk, Maksim Safaniuk. 20–21 – Copter Ural, Elizaveta Galitckaia, f11photo, Manolines, Songquan Deng, Vaclav Matous. 22–23 – JaySi, katalinks, Melinda Fawver, TG Drone Media, Viktar Malyshchyts. 24–25 – Goinyk Production, haspil, PixSaJu, Pommeyrol Vincent, yari2000. 26–27 – Andrei Armiagov, iacomino FRiMAGES, lukaszemanphoto, Vaclav Matous. 28–29 – Akarawut, Robert Kneschke, Tapui, VE.Studio. 30 – Akarawut, BongkarnGraphic.

Bearport Publishing Company Product Development Team
President: Jen Jenson; Director of Product Development: Spencer Brinker; Managing Editor: Allison Juda; Associate Editor: Naomi Reich; Associate Editor: Tiana Tran; Art Director: Colin O'Dea; Designer: Kim Jones; Designer: Kayla Eggert; Product Development Assistant: Owen Hamlin

Library of Congress Cataloging-in-Publication Data is available at www.loc.gov or upon request from the publisher.

ISBN: 979-8-88916-977-2 (hardcover)
ISBN: 979-8-89232-154-9 (ebook)

© 2025 BookLife Publishing
This edition is published by arrangement with BookLife Publishing.

North American adaptations © 2025 Bearport Publishing Company. All rights reserved. No part of this publication may be reproduced in whole or in part, stored in any retrieval system, or transmitted in any form or by any means, electronic, mechanical, photocopying, recording, or otherwise, without written permission from the publisher. Bearport Publishing is a division of Chrysalis Education Group.

For more information, write to Bearport Publishing, 5357 Penn Avenue South, Minneapolis, MN 55419.

CONTENTS

Going Wild 4
To Protect and Restore 6
The Balance of Nature 8
Humanity's Impact 10
The Carbon Cycle 12
Climate Change 14
Forests 16
Wetlands 18
Rivers 20
Floodplains 22
Oceans 24
Biodiversity 26
Who Can Help? 28
A Balancing Act 30
Glossary 31
Index 32
Read More 32
Learn More Online 32

GOING WILD

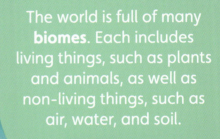

The world is full of many **biomes**. Each includes living things, such as plants and animals, as well as non-living things, such as air, water, and soil.

Everything in a biome is linked together as well as to the wider natural world. A single drop of water can travel far through different parts of nature. A raindrop may fall into a river that flows down a mountain, through a forest, and out into the sea.

Biomes can be incredible. They may include rushing rivers, dense jungles, towering mountains, and deep oceans. However, they can still be damaged by human actions.

People can work together to help the planet.

Today, there are lots of people working hard to repair damage to nature. They're fighting to help Earth and keep all living things healthy.

TO PROTECT AND RESTORE

Warmer arctic temperatures are causing glaciers to melt and crumble.

Nature is made up of delicately balanced **ecosystems**. These are communities of plants and animals that support one another's survival. When any one of these plants or animals becomes sick, the whole community can be threatened.

When an ecosystem's **climate** becomes hotter, colder, wetter, or drier, this can upset its balance. If a landscape becomes **polluted** or taken over by roads and buildings, the ecosystem can be threatened. It may be difficult or impossible for an area's plants and animals to survive.

Pollution poisons both the air and the water that living things need to survive.

Human activity is the leading cause of climate change that can harm nature. But humans can also lead the way toward the **restoration** and protection of nature and its living communities.

The goal of restoration is to return damaged areas to the way they used to be before humans changed them. Protection is about working to keep natural areas safe and unchanged.

THE BALANCE OF NATURE

Nothing in nature exists on its own. Every part of a biome supports the others. The soil, the water, each plant, and the tiniest animal are all a part of the health and survival of the whole community.

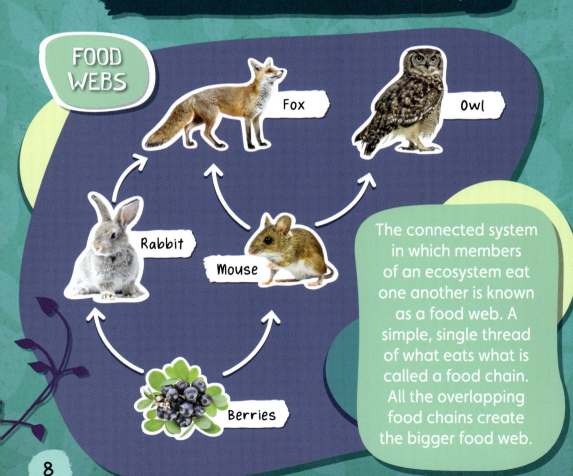

FOOD WEBS

The connected system in which members of an ecosystem eat one another is known as a food web. A simple, single thread of what eats what is called a food chain. All the overlapping food chains create the bigger food web.

LIFE CYCLES

All living things have a life cycle. Animals and plants grow, change, **reproduce**, and die. Each step along the way is important for the survival of a wide variety of **species** of plants and animals.

Eggs

Tadpole

Frog

LANDSCAPE

Landscapes change over time. Oceans wear away at coastlines. Rivers shift direction and carve into dry land. During hot and dry periods, some meadows and woodlands become desert.

If a food web is damaged, animals might not have food to eat. If there is not enough food, living things may not be able to reproduce. If these things cause plants and animals to disappear, the landscape will change and **habitats** can be destroyed.

HUMANITY'S IMPACT

Humanity has used **raw materials** from nature for thousands of years. Firewood and lumber are gathered from trees. Metals and fossil fuels are taken out of the ground. At first, this did not cause lasting harm. However, as human populations became larger and more advanced, we began to cause more and more damage to nature.

Rocks that have useful minerals, such as metals, are called ores.

THE INDUSTRIAL REVOLUTION

The Industrial Revolution started in the 1700s. During this time, people created many new machines to make lots of new things. But in order for the machines to run, they needed fuel.

FOSSIL FUELS

Fossil fuels are found in the ground. They formed over thousands or millions of years from the remains of long-dead plants and animals. During the Industrial Revolution, people discovered that they could power machines by burning coal, a common fossil fuel.

Coal

Oil is also a fossil fuel. It is pumped out of the ground.

Burning coal and oil creates a lot of energy. However, fossil fuels release a gas called carbon dioxide when they are burned. Although carbon dioxide exists naturally in the air, burning fossil fuels puts much more of it into the **atmosphere** than is natural.

11

THE CARBON CYCLE

All plants and animals, including humans, are **carbon**-based organisms, meaning carbon is one of the main **elements** they are made of. Carbon is also stored in the oceans, in the ground, and in the atmosphere. These places are known as carbon sinks.

Carbon naturally moves between carbon sinks as part of something called the carbon cycle. However, human activities have interfered with the carbon cycle.

Burning fossil fuels releases carbon dioxide into the atmosphere.

Some carbon gets stored in the ground.

Just like the other systems in nature, the carbon cycle needs to be balanced. Carbon dioxide is important to life on Earth. In the atmosphere, the gas acts like a blanket, trapping Earth's heat and preventing it from escaping into space. This makes our planet warm enough to support life.

But humans are now pumping too much carbon dioxide into the atmosphere every time we burn fossil fuels. This is changing the balance of the carbon cycle and causing the planet to heat up.

Trees take some carbon dioxide out of the atmosphere.

Some carbon gets stored in the oceans.

CLIMATE CHANGE

Earth's climate has changed many times over millions of years, switching between colder and warmer periods. However, the climate is now changing more quickly than normal. This rapid change has been linked to human activities, mostly the burning of fossil fuels.

THE GREENHOUSE EFFECT

Our planet is warm enough to support life because of the greenhouse effect. The sun's heat hits Earth and warms it up. Some heat bounces back into space. But gases in our planet's atmosphere trap some heat, keeping the planet from freezing.

The sun's heat hits Earth.

Gases in the atmosphere trap some of the heat.

Some heat bounces back to space.

Carbon dioxide is one kind of greenhouse gas. As humans burn more fossil fuels, they put more of these gases into the atmosphere, trapping more heat. This makes the planet even warmer.

Factories release greenhouse gases when they burn fossil fuels.

Rising temperatures are part of a broader pattern of climate change. These changes to the weather affect ecosystems. Areas can become too hot or too cold for the plants and animals that live there. Some habitats may disappear altogether.

Rivers may dry up due to heat and a lack of rain caused by climate change.

FORESTS

Forests are full of trees and many other plants. They are often home to a large variety of animals. These biomes play an important role in balancing the carbon cycle. All the plants help remove carbon dioxide from the atmosphere.

Humans cut down forests for their wood. They also remove trees to make space for farms and buildings. Removing forests is known as deforestation. The practice destroys habitats and damages the balance of the carbon cycle.

Cutting down just one tree affects many animals.

THE PHILIPPINES

The Philippines is an island nation in southeast Asia. In 1900, most of the country was covered in jungles. One hundred years later, however, most of those jungles had been cut down for firewood and timber. Biomes that supported millions of plant and animal species were destroyed.

The Philippine government has created laws to protect the jungles that are left. People are working to replant the trees that were cut down, adding thousands of new trees to restore the lost ecosystems.

A jungle in the Philippines

Rebuilding the Philippines' forests will take decades.

WETLANDS

Wetlands are areas, such as swamps and marshes, where the land is often covered with shallow water. Wetlands can support entire ecosystems with thousands of plant and animal species. The plants there absorb lots of carbon, helping to slow the planet's warming.

Wetland plants absorb lots of excess water when surrounding lands flood. But humans have drained many wetlands. Areas stripped of these ecosystems often flood during heavy rains or high tides.

Digging ditches is one way people drain wetlands.

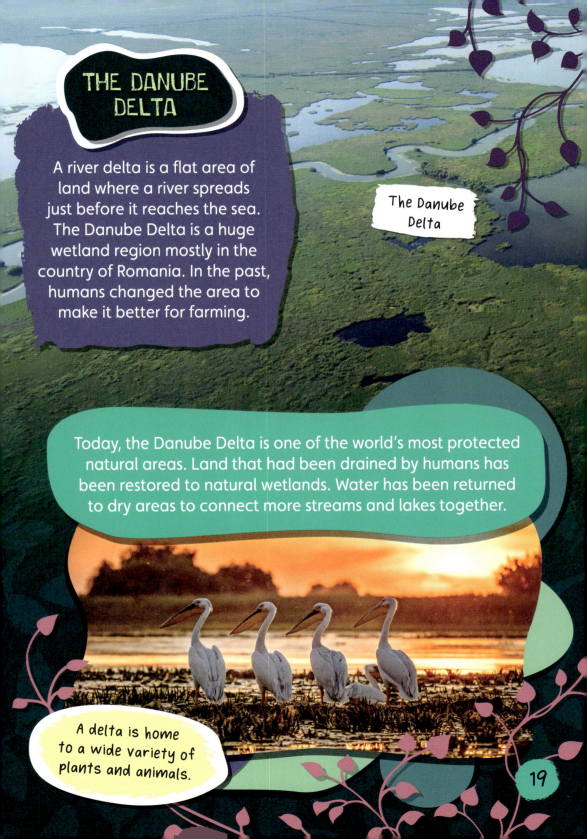

THE DANUBE DELTA

A river delta is a flat area of land where a river spreads just before it reaches the sea. The Danube Delta is a huge wetland region mostly in the country of Romania. In the past, humans changed the area to make it better for farming.

The Danube Delta

Today, the Danube Delta is one of the world's most protected natural areas. Land that had been drained by humans has been restored to natural wetlands. Water has been returned to dry areas to connect more streams and lakes together.

A delta is home to a wide variety of plants and animals.

RIVERS

Rivers are moving streams of water. They flow downhill, often growing larger and joining together with other rivers along the way. They create many habitats and provide drinking water for wildlife.

Humans have long settled near rivers. The waterways provide food, water, and a means of moving people and goods. However, human settlements can sometimes damage river ecosystems.

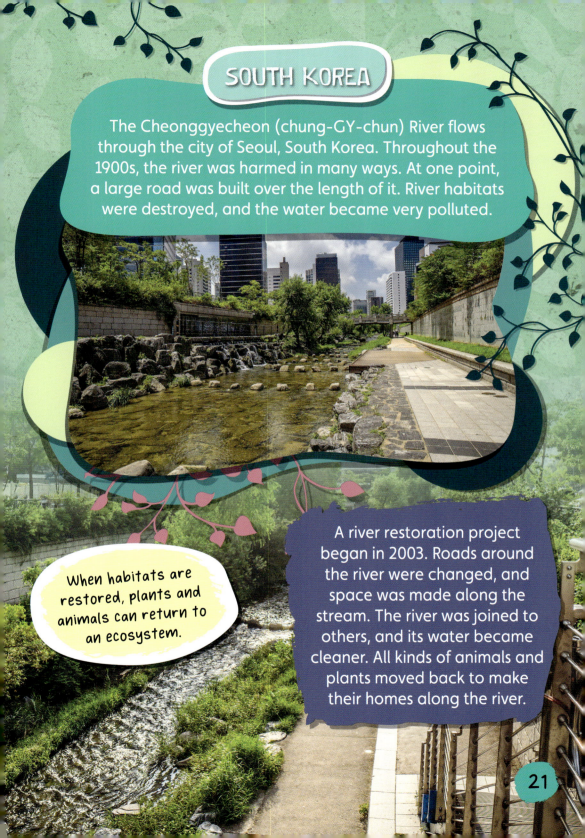

SOUTH KOREA

The Cheonggyecheon (chung-GY-chun) River flows through the city of Seoul, South Korea. Throughout the 1900s, the river was harmed in many ways. At one point, a large road was built over the length of it. River habitats were destroyed, and the water became very polluted.

When habitats are restored, plants and animals can return to an ecosystem.

A river restoration project began in 2003. Roads around the river were changed, and space was made along the stream. The river was joined to others, and its water became cleaner. All kinds of animals and plants moved back to make their homes along the river.

21

FLOODPLAINS

Floodplains are wide stretches of flat land that form naturally alongside rivers. Rivers flood when they have more water than they can hold. The water can collect on floodplains, preventing it from damaging nearby towns, cities, and farmland.

A floodplain

Because floodplains are flat and next to rivers, humans like to build on them. Their rich, well-watered soil makes them good farmland. When humans build or farm on a floodplain, they redirect a river's flow, damaging plant and animal communities throughout the waterway.

THE NETHERLANDS

The Netherlands is a country with a lot of flat land and rivers. For hundreds of years, its people changed how these rivers flowed in order to prevent flooding. But redirecting rivers has also damaged nature and destroyed plant and animal habitats.

People in the Netherlands living along the Meuse River are now allowing the river to flood naturally. This has also allowed lots of wildlife to return to the floodplains along the river.

Meuse River

23

OCEANS

Most of Earth is covered by oceans. Millions of species of plants and animals live in or near these huge bodies of water. Oceans store lots of carbon and keep it out of the atmosphere, where it would trap more of Earth's heat.

Coral reefs are important ocean habitats. They feed and give shelter to millions of plants and sea creatures. But as our planet heats up, so does ocean water. This causes the reefs to die off, threatening all of the sea life in and around them.

Coral reef

Coral reefs and mangrove forests store lots of carbon, keeping it out of the atmosphere.

Mangrove forest

SEAGRASS

Seagrass creates habitats for lots of different fish and sea creatures. It is also an important carbon sink. In some parts of the world, nearly all of the seagrass has been destroyed because of increased pollution and rising temperatures.

Seagrass captures carbon up to 35 times faster than a rainforest.

Luckily, there are groups helping to restore seagrass meadows. They are planting millions of seagrass seeds along coastlines. These new seagrass meadows help feed and provide shelter for wildlife. They also restore some balance to the carbon cycle.

BIODIVERSITY

Most ecosystems include a wide variety of life-forms, including plants, animals, **fungi**, and **microorganisms**. This variety of life is called biodiversity. The mix of many different living things is important for the survival of all.

Hunting and habitat destruction means that there are fewer animals in certain places. If one plant or animal disappears, other animals that rely on them for food or shelter may disappear as well. The loss of biodiversity can even lead to a species going **extinct**.

EURASIAN LYNX

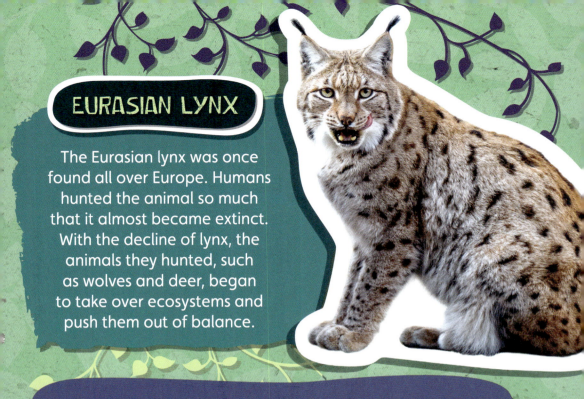

The Eurasian lynx was once found all over Europe. Humans hunted the animal so much that it almost became extinct. With the decline of lynx, the animals they hunted, such as wolves and deer, began to take over ecosystems and push them out of balance.

People have been working hard to protect the Eurasian lynx. Homes have been made for the lynx in places they had once left. Today, thousands of lynx once again live in the wild. Their ecosystems are returning to balance.

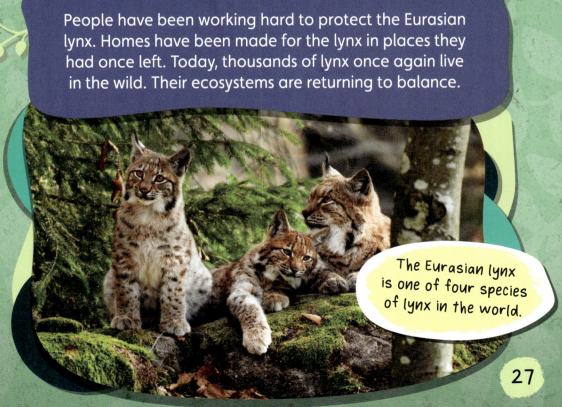

The Eurasian lynx is one of four species of lynx in the world.

Who Can Help?

Habitat protection and restoration projects are done by teams of people. One person cannot do it all, but they can make a difference just by taking part.

Some scientists spend years studying biomes and ecosystems, finding the best ways to protect and restore habitats. Others keep track of different animals to see how they are doing in the wild.

28

You don't need years of training to get involved! Lots of work is done by volunteers who sign up to assist in any way they can. Many parks and nature reserves rely on these volunteers to keep nature healthy.

Think about what you can do in your own yard or garden to protect wildlife and provide a healthy place for plants. You could plant wildflowers to support bees, put up birdhouses, or keep your grass long to feed and give shelter to insects and other small creatures.

Volunteering is a great way to be a part of the solution.

29

A Balancing Act

Protecting wildlife and restoring habitats is all about keeping nature in proper balance. There is a lot of great work being done to heal the parts of nature that have been damaged. But humans still need to live in ways that cause less damage.

If done right, people can still get all the things they need from nature without causing damage. It is all about balance!

Glossary

atmosphere the mixture of gases that make up the air surrounding Earth

biomes areas with certain kinds of land, climate, and living creatures

carbon a natural element found in fossil fuels, such as coal and oil, and in the bodies of living things

climate the usual, expected weather in a certain place

ecosystems communities of living things and the environment they live in

elements substances made from only one type of atom

extinct died off completely

fungi plantlike living things that live on or in plants, animals, or rotting materials

habitats places where plants and animals live or grow

microorganisms tiny, simple life-forms, such as bacteria, algae, and fungi

polluted made dirty or damaged by waste called pollution

raw materials things that humans use that are gathered from nature, such as wood, cotton, and rubber

reproduce to create more of the same kind of life-form

restoration returning something to its natural state

species groups that animals or plants are divided into according to similar characteristics

INDEX

atmosphere 11–16, 24
carbon 11–13, 15–16, 18, 24–25
carbon cycle, the 12–13, 16, 25
climate change 7, 14–15
coral reefs 24
food webs 8–9
fossil fuels 11–15
greenhouse effect, the 14
Industrial Revolution, the 10–11
life cycles 9
oceans 5, 9, 12–13, 20, 24
rivers 4–5, 9, 15, 19–23

READ MORE

Henzel, Cynthia Kennedy. *Using Carbon Sinks to Fight Climate Change (Fighting Climate Change with Science).* Lake Elmo, MN: Focus Readers, 2023.

Knutson, Julie. *Do the Work! Climate Action, Life below Water, and Life on Land (Committing to the UN's Sustainable Development Goals).* Ann Arbor, MI: Cherry Lake Publishing, 2022.

Steen, David A. *Rewilding: Bringing Wildlife Back Where It Belongs.* New York: Neon Squid, 2022.

LEARN MORE ONLINE

1. Go to **www.factsurfer.com** or scan the QR code below.
2. Enter **"Wild Nature"** into the search box.
3. Click on the cover of this book to see a list of websites.